Titanic's Fatal Voyage

by Kevin Blake

Consultant: Melinda E. Ratchford, EdD
Titanic Historian and Associate Professor
Sister Christine Beck Department of Education
Belmont Abbey College
Belmont, North Carolina

BEARPORT
PUBLISHING

New York, New York

Credits

Cover, Titanic Painting © Ken Marschall; 4T, Library of Congress; 4–5, Titanic Painting © Ken Marschall; 6T, © Mary Evans/ National Archives/The Image Works; 6B, Harland & Wolff Shipyard/tinyurl.com/ydb4xpmk/public domain; 7T, Wikimedia/ tinyurl.com/y7jpbwej/public domain; 7B, © Photo by Michel Boutefeu/Getty Images; 8T, © Photo by David Paul Morris/Getty Images; 8B, © United Archives GmbH/Alamy; 9, © akg-images/Newscom; 10T, Wikimedia/tinyurl.com/ybkrqkgn/public domain; 10B, © akg-images/The Image Works; 11, Library of Congress; 12–13, © SZ Photo/Scherl/The Image Works; 13R, © akg-images/ Universal Images Gr/The Image Works; 14–15, Titanic Painting © Ken Marschall; 15T, © United Archives GmbH/Alamy; 16, Titanic Painting © Ken Marschall; 17, Titanic Painting © Ken Marschall; 18T, Titanic Painting © Ken Marschall; 18B, Titanic Painting © Ken Marschall; 19T, Titanic Painting © Ken Marschall; 19B, Bernard Walker Dodd, Mead and Company, New York/tinyurl.com/ycp77r6r/ public domain; 20T, © The Titanic Collection/Universal Images Group/age fotostock; 20B, © Dorling Kindersley/Getty Images; 21, © Chronicle/Alamy; 22L, © tc_2/Getty Images; 22R, © Chronicle/Alamy; 23, Wikimedia/tinyurl.com/y7gu2bsh/public domain; 24– 25, Titanic Painting © Ken Marschall; 26T, Wikimedia/tinyurl.com/y75qgfy9/public domain; 26B, © tc_2/Getty Images; 27, © ZUMA PRESS/Moviestills/age fotostock; 28TL, europeana newspapers/tinyurl.com/ycob2mrd/CC BY-SA 2.0; 28BL, europeana newspapers/ tinyurl.com/y9lg9f27/CC BY-SA 2.0; 28R, © Pictorial Press Ltd/Alamy; 29T, © Heritage Image Partnership Ltd/Alamy; 29BL, © Lebrecht Music and Arts Photo Library/Alamy; 28BR, © Mary Evans Picture Library/ONSLOW AUCTIONS LIMITED/Mary Evans Picture Library Ltd/age fotostock; 31, Library of Congress; 32, © akg-images/Newscom.

Publisher: Kenn Goin
Senior Editor: Joyce Tavolacci
Creative Director: Spencer Brinker
Design: Dawn Beard Creative
Photo Researcher: Editorial Directions, Inc.

Library of Congress Cataloging-in-Publication Data

Names: Blake, Kevin, 1978- author.
Title: Titanic's fatal voyage / by Kevin Blake.
Description: New York, New York : Bearport Publishing Company, Inc., 2018. | Series: Titanica | Includes bibliographical references and index.
Identifiers: LCCN 2017045550 (print) | LCCN 2017046187 (ebook) | ISBN 9781684024902 (ebook) | ISBN 9781684024322 (library)
Subjects: LCSH: Titanic (Steamship)—Juvenile literature. | Shipwrecks—North Atlantic Ocean—Juvenile literature.
Classification: LCC G530.T6 (ebook) | LCC G530.T6 B594 2018 (print) | DDC 910.9163/4—dc23
LC record available at https://lccn.loc.gov/2017045550

For more information, write to Bearport Publishing Company, Inc., 45 West 21st Street, Suite 3B, New York, New York 10011. Printed in the United States of America.

10 9 8 7 6 5 4 3 2 1

CONTENTS

ICEBERG AHEAD!

It was nearly midnight on April 14, 1912. Frederick Fleet, a **lookout** on the RMS *Titanic*, stared out into the dark ocean and starlit sky. His warm breath made white puffs in the **frigid** air. The water was so calm, it looked like glass. Then he noticed something. Was it mist on the water? Suddenly, a huge mountain of ice as tall as a six-story building appeared.

Frederick Fleet, one of the *Titanic*'s lookouts

The RMS *Titanic*

Frederick **frantically** rang a warning bell and called down to the officers steering the ship. "Iceberg, right ahead!" he yelled. The officers shut off the engines and steered the gigantic ship to the left as quickly as they could. The *Titanic* began to slowly turn—but it was already too late. There was a grinding sound as the ship scraped against the giant iceberg. One of the world's greatest **disasters** was about to unfold.

The *Titanic* struck the iceberg less than a minute after Frederick Fleet's warning.

SHIP OF DREAMS

Five years earlier, the *Titanic* began as one man's incredible dream. His name was J. Bruce Ismay. As the **chairman** of the White Star Line, a British shipping company, Ismay wanted to create the biggest, fastest, and most **luxurious** ship the world had ever seen.

J. Bruce Ismay

At the time, the *Titanic* would be the largest moving object ever built!

It took two years and thousands of workers to carry out Ismay's vision. When the *Titanic* was completed, the huge ship was almost as long as three football fields and as wide as a four-lane highway. To make it extra strong, the bottom of the ship's **hull** was covered with two layers of **steel** plates. In addition, there were 16 **compartments** inside the *Titanic*'s hull, each separated by a special door. If water got into a compartment, the doors would stop it from reaching other parts of the ship. The *Titanic* was considered unsinkable.

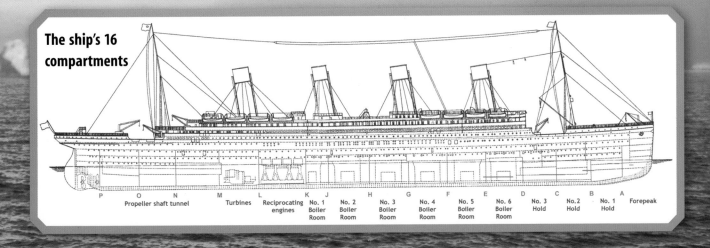

The ship's 16 compartments

P · O · N · M · L · K J H G F E D C B A
Propeller shaft tunnel · Turbines · Reciprocating engines · No. 1 Boiler Room · No. 2 Boiler Room · No. 3 Boiler Room · No. 4 Boiler Room · No. 5 Boiler Room · No. 6 Boiler Room · No. 3 Hold · No. 2 Hold · No. 1 Hold · Forepeak

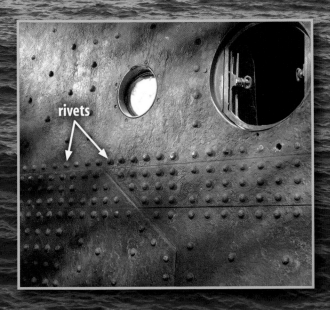

rivets

Three million rivets— or metal bolts— attached the steel plates to the ship's hull.

Even if four of the compartments filled with water, the *Titanic* would still be able to float.

Luxury or Safety?

After it was completed, the *Titanic* was as luxurious as Ismay had dreamt. It had a swimming pool, several restaurants, and large rooms for its wealthy **first-class** passengers. The ship also had three **elevators** and a grand staircase lit by a domed **skylight**.

What the *Titanic*'s grand staircase might have looked like

One of the ship's fancy dining rooms

The *Titanic's* **architect** planned for the ship to carry 48 lifeboats—enough for everyone on board. However, storing so many boats would mean less space on the **deck** for the first-class passengers to enjoy. Ismay decided to drastically cut the number of lifeboats. Now, the *Titanic* would carry only 20 boats, enough for only about 1,200 people—or about half the people on the ship.

More lifeboats meant less open space for wealthy passengers to view the ocean.

The *Titanic's* plan originally extended the height of each of the 16 compartments almost to the top of the ship. This design, too, was changed because the compartments would take away space from the first-class dining room.

Excited Passengers

On April 10, 1912, the world's largest ship was ready to set sail for New York. Excited passengers boarded the *Titanic* in Southampton, England. The ship would then sail to France and Ireland to pick up additional passengers. The ship's captain, Edward J. Smith, personally greeted each traveler in first class. The first-class passengers included millionaires, such as businessman John Jacob Astor IV and Isidor and Ida Straus, the owners of Macy's department store. They were returning to America after a European vacation.

Captain
Edward J. Smith

The *Titanic* in
Southampton, England

Most of the approximately 1,300 passengers were not rich, however. More than half had purchased the least expensive third-class tickets. These people came from all over Europe to seek a better life in America. As the *Titanic* left **port**, everyone—from the richest **tycoon** to the poorest **immigrant**—was thrilled. They had no idea of the nightmare that was to come.

There were more than 100 children traveling on the *Titanic*, enough that the White Star Line, the ship's owners, provided a library just for them.

Second-class passengers Marjorie Collyer (age eight) and her mother, Charlotte "Lottie" Collyer

A Bad Omen

Disaster almost struck the *Titanic* minutes after it left Southampton. Because of its huge size, the *Titanic* created large waves as it pulled out of its **slip**. The waves caused a nearby ship called the *New York* to bob violently in the water.

New York

tugboat

A tugboat tries to pull the *New York* away from the larger *Titanic*.

Suddenly, several earsplitting bangs rang out. Six heavy ropes that held the *New York* to the dock snapped. The much smaller ship then swung out toward the side of the *Titanic*. Passengers watched in fear as the ships came within inches of smashing into each other. "It was a close call," said a captain of a nearby tugboat. It was also a terrible **omen** for a ship about to cross the vast Atlantic Ocean for the very first time.

Titanic

A photo taken aboard the *Titanic* shows how close the ship came to crashing into the *New York*.

The *Titanic* was so huge that it **displaced** a lot of water as it moved, creating a huge **wake**.

FULL STEAM AHEAD!

As the *Titanic* sped on its **maiden voyage** through the waters of the northern Atlantic Ocean, its radio operators began receiving warnings from other ships. There was danger ahead. One ship reported a "great number [of] large icebergs" directly in the *Titanic*'s path. Crashing into any of them could mean serious trouble for the ship.

Captain Smith had a choice to make. He could keep the *Titanic* moving at nearly full speed or slow the ship down to give the crew more time to spot the icebergs. However, this option meant that the ship might not arrive in New York on time. Captain Smith chose to maintain the ship's speed—even as additional ice warnings from other ships poured in.

A photograph of the icy waters that the *Titanic* sailed through in April 1912

The *Titanic* moved toward New York City at a speed of 22.5 knots (26 mph). If the ship continued at that speed, it would arrive a day early.

SUDDEN IMPACT

Captain Smith's decision was a deadly mistake. At 11:40 PM—about a minute after Frederick Fleet spotted the iceberg—the *Titanic* collided with it. Deep under the dark ocean water, the giant base of the iceberg scraped the boat's steel skin, badly damaging it. Immediately, water began to pour inside the ship.

After the crash, the ship's officers closed the doors between the special compartments. The *Titanic* could stay afloat with four of its compartments flooded. However, the crash had caused six to flood.

What it might have looked like from the front of the ship, heading toward the iceberg

For many passengers, the crash felt like nothing more than a little bump. Captain Smith, who was jolted awake by the accident, knew it was more than that. He immediately woke up Thomas Andrews, the *Titanic's* architect. They both rushed below deck to check the damage and found water gushing into the hull. A frightened Andrews guessed that the *Titanic* would sink in less than two hours. Captain Smith had to take action. Thousands of lives depended on it.

The flooded compartments would weigh down the front of the ship, causing it to sink.

©KEN MARSCHALL 1992

TO THE LIFEBOATS!

Boom, boom, boom! The crew shot rockets into the air to alert nearby ships that the *Titanic* was in trouble. They also sent out **distress signals** over the radio. "Come at once. We have struck a berg!" read one message. Captain Smith ordered the crew to prepare the lifeboats. Other crew members pounded on doors to wake up sleeping passengers. The guests were told to hurry to the lifeboats on one of the ship's decks.

The *Titanic* fired several distress rockets.

This painting shows crew members directing passengers to the lifeboat deck.

©KEN MARS... 1992

Meanwhile, there was **chaos** deep in the hull of the ship. More than seven tons (6 mt) of water surged into the ship every second. The crew desperately tried to pump the water out, but it poured in fifteen times faster than the pumps could handle. Third-class passengers struggled to make their way through a maze of flooded passageways to the ship's lifeboat deck.

When the *Titanic*'s officers explained the plan to board the lifeboats, several passengers simply refused. One first-class traveler replied, "We are safer here than in that little boat."

The crew tried to pump the cold ocean water away from the *Titanic*'s hot boilers. If the water touched a boiler, it could have caused a huge explosion.

Titanic's boilers

WOMEN AND CHILDREN FIRST

Captain Smith ordered women and children to board the lifeboats first. The crew scrambled to carry out his order. If they didn't see any women and children nearby, some crew members lowered lifeboats into the ocean with empty seats. When John Jacob Astor IV helped his wife, Madeleine, into a lifeboat, the crew wouldn't give him a seat even though there were twenty empty ones.

John J. Astor and his wife, Madeleine

As the ship's **bow** began to dip down into the **treacherous** water, Charlotte "Lottie" Collyer and other wives begged their husbands to join them on the lifeboats. Lottie's husband, Harvey, yelled to his wife, "Go, Lottie! For God's sake, be brave and go! I'll get a seat in another boat!" Harvey would soon drown.

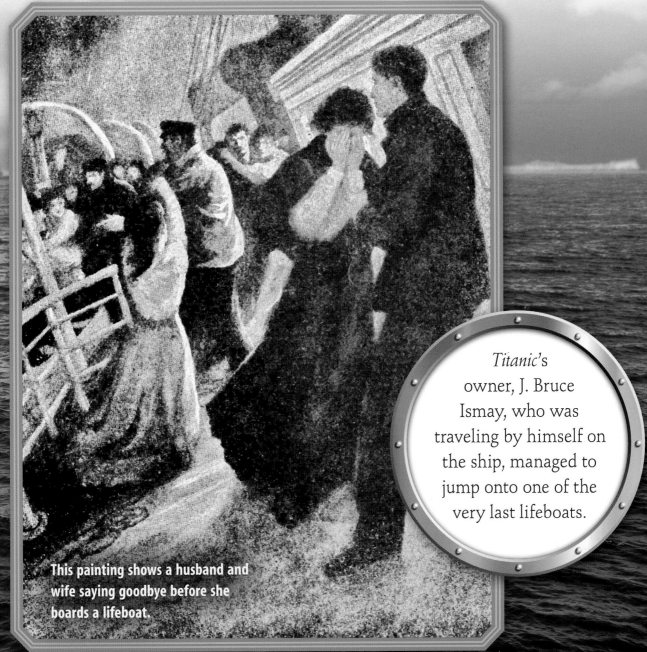

This painting shows a husband and wife saying goodbye before she boards a lifeboat.

Titanic's owner, J. Bruce Ismay, who was traveling by himself on the ship, managed to jump onto one of the very last lifeboats.

DOWN WITH THE SHIP

As the mighty *Titanic* continued its **descent** into the icy Atlantic, it became clear to many that there was little chance for **survival**. Some people **panicked**. A few men tried to force their way onto full lifeboats. Others jumped off the sinking ship into the lifeboats, crushing people as they landed. Officer Harold Lowe fired a warning shot in the air to maintain order on the deck.

Officer Harold Lowe

To try and keep passengers calm, the *Titanic*'s orchestra played lively tunes up until the ship sank.

Other passengers sadly accepted their fate. Some couples chose to stay together. Ida Straus refused to leave her husband Isidor's side, saying simply, "Where you go, I go." Alfred Rush, age 16, was offered a place on a lifeboat. He firmly said, "No, I'm staying here with the men."

Titanic passengers in a lifeboat

SWALLOWED BY THE SEA

Around 2:20 AM, the *Titanic's* **propellers** lifted out of the ocean. There were no more lifeboats, and more than 1,500 helpless people remained on the ship. Some passengers and crew decided to jump into the icy sea. Many died in the freezing water, which was less than 28°F (-2°C). Amazingly, Officer Charles Lightoller survived the jump. When he landed in the bitterly cold ocean, however, it felt like "a thousand knives" had stabbed his body.

The *Titanic* sank at 2:20 AM on April 15, 1912. It took 2 hours and 40 minutes for the great ship to fully sink.

Minutes later, the people who had stayed on the ship were washed into the sea. Many immediately died from **hypothermia**. The *Titanic* then let out a groan like a dying animal and slipped under the water. Captain Smith went down with his ship.

More than 1,500 people would die during the disaster—or more than half of the *Titanic*'s passengers and crew.

RESCUED!

In the very early morning of April 15, *Titanic's* survivors first **glimpsed** the twinkling lights of a rescue ship, the *Carpathia*. "We caught sight of the port light of *Carpathia*, and knew that we were saved," said one survivor. The ship had received the *Titanic's* call for help and sped through a maze of icebergs to reach the site of the disaster.

The rescue ship *Carpathia*

An illustration showing a group of rescuers

For more than four hours, the *Carpathia*'s crew worked rescuing more than 700 freezing survivors. As the *Carpathia* started its engines and headed for New York, shivering women lined the ship's railing. They desperately searched the waters for their lost husbands, fathers, and sons. Tears streamed down their faces as they realized they would never see their loved ones again. People all over the world would soon learn about the *Titanic* tragedy—and forever be haunted by the greatest sea disaster in history.

In 1985, underwater explorers discovered the *Titanic* wreck on the ocean floor.

The *Titanic* on the floor of the Atlantic Ocean

THE WORLD REACTS
TO THE *TITANIC* DISASTER

When the *Titanic* sank on April 15, 1912, the world reacted with shock, disbelief, and sadness. The greatest sea disaster in history created an outpouring of news stories, personal responses, and books.

Newspapers around the world covered the terrible tragedy.

Crowds gather in New York City to learn about the sinking of the *Titanic*.

King George V and Queen Mary

Upon hearing of the ship's fate, King George V of England sent a message to the White Star Line, the company that owned the *Titanic*.

"The Queen and I are horrified at the appalling disaster which has happened to the Titanic *and at the terrible loss of life."*

—King George V

The very same year the *Titanic* sank, several books about the ship were written, including *The Sinking of the Titanic and Great Sea Disasters*, edited by Logan Marshall.

"The Titanic, *greatest of ships, has gone to her ocean grave."*

—The Sinking of the Titanic and Great Sea Disasters

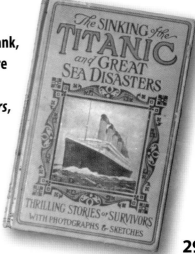

GLOSSARY

architect (AR-ki-tekt) someone who designs large objects like buildings or ships

bow (BOU) the front of the ship

chairman (CHAIR-muhn) the head of a business or organization

chaos (KAY-oss) confusion that creates disorder or panic

compartments (kuhm-PAHRT-muhnts) separate sections of something

deck (DEK) an upper floor of a ship

descent (dih-SENT) the process of moving lower

disasters (dih-ZAS-turz) horrible events

displaced (dis-PLAYST) moved from one place to another

distress signals (dih-STRESS SIG-nuhls) signs used to alert others to a problem

elevators (EL-uh-vay-turz) moving platforms that carry people or freight from one level to another

first-class (FURST-KLASS) the highest or best quality

frantically (FRAN-tik-lee) wild with fear or excitement

frigid (FRIJ-id) extremely cold

glimpsed (GLIMPSD) looked at briefly

hull (HUHL) the lowermost portion of a ship

hypothermia (hye-puh-THUR-mee-uh) the condition of having dangerously low body temperature

immigrant (IM-uh-gruhnt) a person who leaves one country to live in another

lookout (LUK-out) someone who keeps watch for objects or people

luxurious (luhk-SHUH-ree-uhss) fancy and comfortable

maiden voyage (MAYD-uhn VOI-ij) the first trip of a ship

omen (OH-muhn) a sign of things to come

panicked (PAN-ikt) felt extreme fear or terror

port (PORT) a place where ships load and unload passengers and goods

propellers (pruh-PEL-uhrz) devices with spinning blades that help move a ship

skylight (SKY-lite) a window in a roof or ceiling

slip (SLIP) a landing place for ships

steel (STEEL) a hard, strong metal used for making objects and buildings

survival (sur-VYE-vuhl) the act of staying alive

treacherous (TRECH-ur-uhss) dangerous

tycoon (tye-KOON) a person with great wealth

wake (WAYK) waves left by a ship

BIBLIOGRAPHY

Eaton, John P., and Charles A. Haas. *Titanic: Triumph and Tragedy.* New York: W. W. Norton & Co. (1995).

Green, Rod. *Building the Titanic: An Epic Tale of the Creation of History's Most Famous Ocean Liner.* New York: Reader's Digest (2005).

READ MORE

Blake, Kevin. *Creating Titanic: The Ship of Dreams (Titanica).* New York: Bearport (2018).

Giannini, Alex. *Titanic's Passengers and Crew (Titanica).* New York: Bearport (2018).

Goldish, Meish. *Titanic's Last Hours: The Facts (Titanica).* New York: Bearport (2018).

LEARN MORE ONLINE

To learn more about the *Titanic*'s fatal voyage, visit
www.bearportpublishing.com/Titanica

INDEX

ABOUT THE AUTHOR

Kevin Blake lives in Providence, Rhode Island, with his wife, Melissa, his son, Sam, and his daughter, Ilana. He has written more than 20 books for young readers.